Cockapoos

by Ruth Owen

PowerKiDS
press

New York

Published in 2013 by The Rosen Publishing Group, Inc.
29 East 21st Street, New York, NY 10010

First Edition

Produced for Rosen by Ruby Tuesday Books Ltd
Editor for Ruby Tuesday Books Ltd: Mark J. Sachner
US Editor: Sara Antill
Designer: Emma Randall

Photo Credits:
Cover, 1, 3, 4–5, 6–7, 8–9, 10–11, 12–13, 14, 16–17, 18–19, 20–21, 24–25, 28,
30 © Shutterstock; 15, 27 © FLPA; 22 © Ardea; 23 © Istock; 29 © Cockapoo
Club of GB/Matt Nuttall Photography.

Library of Congress Cataloging-in-Publication Data

Owen, Ruth, 1967–
 Cockapoos / by Ruth Owen. — 1st ed.
   p. cm. — (Designer dogs)
Includes index.
 ISBN 978-1-4488-7855-0 (library binding) — ISBN 978-1-4488-7908-3 (pbk.)
— ISBN 978-1-4488-7914-4 (6-pack)
1. Cockapoo—Juvenile literature. I. Title.
 SF429.C54O94 2013
 636.76—dc23

                                   2012004333

Manufactured in the United States of America

CPSIA Compliance Information: Batch #B1S12PK: For Further Information contact Rosen Publishing, New York, New York at 1-800-237-9932

Contents

woof

Meet a Cockapoo

What is smart and happy, loves to cuddle, and has wavy or curly hair? It's a cockapoo!

Cockapoos are a **crossbreed** dog. This means they are a mixture of two different **breeds**, or types, of dog. When a cocker spaniel and a poodle have puppies together, they make cockapoos!

Cockapoos are real "people" dogs. As long as they are with their owners, they are happy.

Adult cocker spaniel

Adult poodle

Cockapoo puppy

Cockapoos are known as "designer dogs" because **dog breeders** designed, or created, them by mating two other breeds. Cockapoos were first bred in the 1950s.

An adult cockapoo

Sneeze-Free Pups

Many people get ill around dogs because they have an **allergy** to them.

Most dogs shed, or drop, lots of hair. The hair carries tiny bits of dead skin called dander. When people with an allergy get near dog hair or dander, they may sneeze or become ill.

Poodle hair doesn't drop out, however, and it doesn't make allergic people ill. Crossbreed dogs, such as cockapoos, that have a poodle parent usually have this type of hair, too. Many people with a dog allergy do not get sick when they are around a cockapoo.

A cockapoo

Cockapoos are not the only
sneeze-free crossbreed dogs.
- Poodle + Labrador retriever = labradoodle
- Poodle + golden retriever = goldendoodle
- Poodle + schnauzer = schnoodle

A schnoodle

A goldendoodle

A labradoodle

Meet the Parents: Cocker Spaniels

A cockapoo may have an American or an English cocker spaniel as a parent.

Cocker spaniels have silky, wavy hair. Their coats can be black, brown, red, cream, or golden. Sometimes cocker spaniels are one of these colors mixed with white. They may also have small patches of tan, a pale brown color, on their heads.

Cocker spaniels are **compact** little dogs with **sturdy** bodies.

Adult American cocker spaniel size

Height to shoulder = 13 to 15 inches (33 to 38 cm)

A golden cocker spaniel

Cocker spaniels are fast runners. They also have good endurance. This means they can run and be active for a long time without getting tired.

Two brown cocker spaniels

Meet the Parents: Working Cocker Spaniels

Cocker spaniels were originally bred to be working dogs. They helped their owners hunt birds and other small animals.

A cocker spaniel's job was to search for **prey** in bushes and long grass. The dog would flush, or drive, the prey animal out into the open so that the dog's owner could shoot it. Then the dog would retrieve the dead prey and carry it back to its master.

American cocker spaniel puppies

There are several types of spaniel. Cocker spaniels got their name because they were used to hunt birds called woodcocks.

A cocker spaniel retrieving a bird

Meet the Parents: Poodles

Poodles are extremely smart dogs that find it easy to learn new things.

Poodles come in different sizes, but they are all the same breed. There are standard (large) poodles, miniature poodles, and toy poodles. Cockapoos usually have a miniature or toy poodle parent.

A poodle's coat might be black, brown, red, gray, silver, white, cream, or apricot.

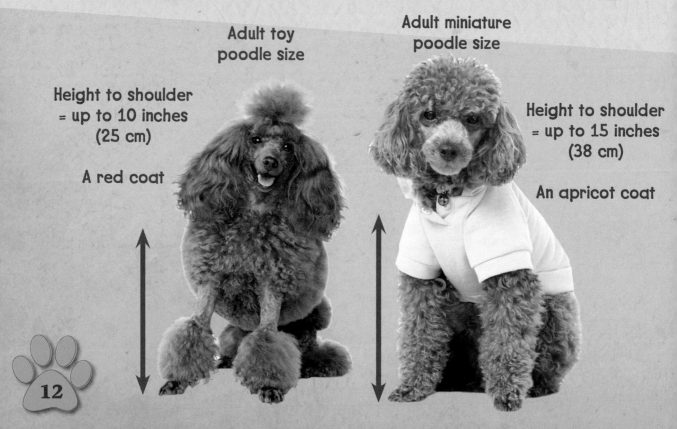

Adult toy poodle size

Adult miniature poodle size

Height to shoulder = up to 10 inches (25 cm)

A red coat

Height to shoulder = up to 15 inches (38 cm)

An apricot coat

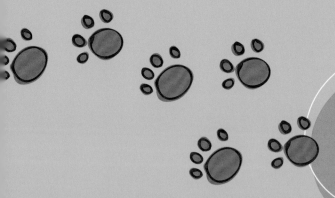

If a poodle's woolly, curly hair is not clipped, or cut, it can grow into cords that look like dreadlocks!

A black poodle

Meet the Parents: Working Poodles

Like cocker spaniels, poodles were originally bred to be working dogs. They helped their owners hunt water birds, such as ducks.

Poodles love to be in water, and they are excellent swimmers. So when a hunter shot a bird, the poodle would dive into the pond or lake to retrieve the dead bird. Then the dog would carry the bird back to its owner.

A one-week-old poodle puppy

It's believed that poodles were first bred in Germany. Their name comes from a German word, "pudel." The word means "splashing in water."

Cockapoo Looks

Some cockapoos look like their cocker spaniel parent, while others look more like a poodle. That's one of the great things about crossbreed dogs. They can have lots of different looks!

If a cockapoo has a miniature poodle parent, it will normally be a miniature cockapoo. A toy poodle parent will create a toy cockapoo.

Adult toy cockapoo

Height to shoulder = up to 10 inches (25.4 cm)

Adult miniature cockapoo

Height to shoulder = 11 to 14 inches (28 to 36 cm)

Cockapoos usually live for 14 to 18 years. Some cockapoos have lived for more than 20 years, though!

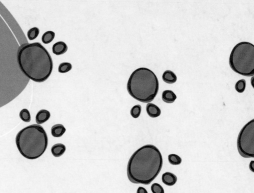

A senior cockapoo

17

Cockapoo Coats

With such colorful parents, it's not surprising that cockapoos come in lots of different colors.

A cockapoo's coat can be black, white, cream, apricot, red, or a chocolate brown color. It might have white patches, or be another color mixed with white.

A cockapoo might have wavy hair like its cocker spaniel parent, have tight curls like a poodle, or be somewhere in between.

Beard

Adult cockapoos need to have their coat brushed two to three times a week. Some owners trim their dog's beard, too. This avoids wet kisses if the dog has been drinking from its water bowl!

A red and white
cockapoo puppy

Cockapoos with Personality

Like their poodle parents, cockapoos are very intelligent. They are easy to train, and they like to show off the things they've learned.

Cockapoos aren't shy dogs. They are outgoing and curious. They like to meet new people and check out new things.

Mostly, however, cockapoos just want to be around the people they love. Being with their owner and getting and giving cuddles is the best thing in the world!

Fun at the beach

A cockapoo is happy living with a single person or with a big, noisy family.

Fun in the snow

Cockapoo Pups

A cockapoo can have a cocker spaniel mother and a poodle father, or the other way around. The mother dog usually gives birth to a **litter** of up to six puppies.

The newborn puppies cannot walk, and their eyes are closed. All the little puppies do is sleep and drink milk from their mother. The puppies' eyes open when they are about two weeks old.

By the time the pups are four weeks old, they are walking and playing with their brothers and sisters.

A cockapoo family

A three-week-old
cockapoo puppy

At four weeks old, puppies start
to try out important doggie skills
such as barking and wagging
their tails.

Learning to Be a Dog

Like all puppies, cockapoos should stay with their mothers and brothers and sisters until they are at least eight weeks old. Puppies learn important lessons from their dog family. For example, if a puppy bites its mother, she will let the puppy know that's not okay. That is how a puppy learns not to bite.

Play fighting and chasing with its brothers and sisters helps a puppy learn how to use its body. It's like you playing a sport!

A puppy soon grows bigger and bigger. While it may look like an adult, young dogs still act and think like puppies until they are about two years old.

Cockapoo Hearing Dogs

Some cockapoos use their intelligence and love of people to work as hearing dogs.

A hearing dog lives with a person who is deaf. The dog is trained to touch its owner with its nose or paw if it hears an important sound. The dog might also lead its owner to the sound.

Hearing dogs tell their owners when they hear the doorbell or telephone ring, or the oven timer goes off.

Hearing dogs keep their owners safe by alerting them if a smoke alarm goes off in their owner's home or work place.

A hearing dog cockapoo hurries to let it's owner know that someone's at the front door!

Cockapoo Agility

Dog agility is a fun activity in which dogs have to run around an obstacle course in the quickest possible time. Some cockapoos take part in this sport.

Agility dogs jump over hurdles, weave in and out of poles, and crawl through tunnels. Dog owners run around the course with their pets to give instructions and support.

Dog agility is a team effort between a dog and its owner—just right for people-loving cockapoos!

A tunnel and balance obstacle

A dog agility seesaw

One of the obstacles on a dog agility course is the seesaw. The dog must use its balance to walk up the seesaw, tip it over, and walk down the other side.

An agility cockapoo jumps a hurdle

A cockapoo weaves between poles.

29

Glossary

allergy (A-lur-jee) When a person's body reacts badly to something, such as an animal or type of food. An allergy may make a person sneeze, get sore skin, vomit, or fall seriously ill.

breed (BREED) A type of dog. Also, the word used to describe the act of mating two dogs in order for them to have puppies.

compact (KOM-pakt) Something that does not take up much space and is neat and tightly packed together.

crossbreed
(KROS-breed) A type
of dog created from
two different breeds.

dog breeder
(DAWG BREED-er)
A person who breeds
dogs and sells them.

litter (LIH-ter) A group
of baby animals all born
to the same mother at the
same time.

prey (PRAY) An animal
that is hunted by another
animal as food.

sturdy (STUR-dee)
Something strong and
well built.

toy (TOY) The word
used to describe the
size of a dog that is
very small.

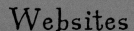

Websites

Due to the changing nature
of Internet links, PowerKids Press has
developed an online list of websites related to the
subject of this book. This site is updated regularly.
Please use this link to access the list:

www.powerkidslinks.com/ddog/cockapoo/

Read More

Landau, Elaine. *Poodles Are the Best!*. Best Dogs Ever. Minneapolis, MN: Lerner Publications, 2010.

Schweitzer, Karen. *The Cocker Spaniel*. Our Best Friends. Pittsburgh, PA: Eldorado Ink, 2011.

Wheeler, Jill C. *Cockapoos*. Minneapolis, MN: Checkerboard Books, 2008.

Index